CONTEMPORARY HOUSE

CONTEMPORARY HOUSE

Janetta Hutchinson

This is a Parragon Publishing Book
This edition published in 2004

Parragon Publishing
Queen Street House
4 Queen Street
Bath BA1 1HE, UK

A copy of the CIP data for this book is available from the British
Library upon request.

ISBN 1-84273-530-6

Printed in China

CONTENTS

INTRODUCTION

The contemporary house is a joy to behold. Bright, light, uncluttered, and clean, these sparsely furnished, minimally decorated rooms are fascinating in their simplicity. Deceptive too, because at first glance there doesn't seem to be much actually to look at within them. In most of the rooms you could almost count the pieces of furniture on the fingers of one hand. But the contemporary house has turned this utilitarian approach to decorating on its head, and what has been designed primarily for use has also resulted in something of beauty. We are able to admire what in one sense amounts to very little because each basic element in the rooms is exquisite in its own right.

The contemporary house doesn't boast any particularly complicated color schemes or offer much in the way of pattern or design to ponder over, and it supplies a mere scattering of accessories to appreciate, but this minimal approach is exactly what gives such a house its unique appeal. People appreciate its understated elegance and absence of clutter, particularly as an antidote to and escape from their often cluttered, hectic lives. The hard surfaces, utilitarian materials, and strong sense of design mean that the contemporary house catches your eye and also your imagination.

The maxim "less is more" sums up the whole attitude toward the contemporary house. Its apparently simple interior design is actually well thought out and cleverly put together, combining modern furniture, interesting textures, and streamlined designs in a way that defies convention.

Inspiration is drawn from the school of minimalism, but without taking it to an extreme. As much emphasis is placed on choosing materials for the walls, floors, and windows as on choosing the furniture. Furthermore, the contemporary house also takes its inspiration from outside the home, bringing office, factory, and industrial fabrics, materials, and ideas indoors. Stainless steel, glass, brick, plastic, and plywood can all be found in these modern homes, often used in places for which they were not originally intended. These modern materials are given pride of place in the interior

where their unique contribution to the decoration of the home can be properly admired.

The ethos of the contemporary house is that rooms can evolve and change, and in many homes the walls have given way to an open-plan layout. The rigidity of traditional design ideas where each room has a single purpose has been dismissed—the idea behind the contemporary house is that each room can fit several briefs. A dining area may not just be for eating and entertaining; it can also be a place that adults use as a home office, where children do their homework, and where hobbies and crafts can be carried out. As such, living spaces within the contemporary home are transient. One large area can accommodate both a living and dining area, and may even make way for a home office or cooking space. This ever-changing concept of space is particularly suitable for many of today's small houses, where accommodating living/dining/office space in the traditional way is often difficult. Fluidity is one of the main concepts of the contemporary house. Boundaries have come down, so one large area can fulfill the job of

several rooms. Demarcation of these areas is achieved in a beautifully
subtle way rather than with the rigidity of walls or permanent barriers.
The use of lighting, for example, can mark boundaries, changing from
low level in living or sleeping areas to bright in work or food-
preparation spaces. Color can denote the change of use of space within
a room, as can the type of flooring used throughout the area.

In some contemporary homes the traditional order of the house has been altered. Living rooms may be found upstairs while sleeping areas may be situated downstairs, especially if a good view is to be afforded from the upper floors, or perhaps more privacy. This rearrangement of room order is not only very useful, but also quite enterprising, as rethinking and restructuring the way in which the interior is used play an important part in the design of the contemporary house.

Much of the furniture used in the contemporary house draws inspiration from landmarks of 20th-century design, and some of the most familiar modern items have an illustrious history. The German school of architecture and design known as the Bauhaus was founded in 1919 and closed down only 14 years later, yet it was the most influential design school of the 20th century and remains a major influence in interior design today. Its ethos was to fuse art, design, architecture, and crafts into a unified whole, and many of its principles are still being implemented in furniture design today. The German architect and designer Mies van der Rohe was a director of the Bauhaus, and his cantilever chair design is over 75 years old; however, this style of chair is ever popular in the contemporary house. Likewise, the French architect Le Corbusier also designed furniture in the 1920s, and his "Grand Confort" armchair, designed in 1928, consisted of large, soft cushions fitted inside a frame made of tubular steel. Today metal and tubular steel furniture is a stalwart of the contemporary house. In 1952 the Danish architect and designer Arne Jacobsen designed the "3107" chair. The backrest and seat were made from one piece of molded plywood, supported by legs of tubular steel. Originally produced just in black, it was later available in a range of colors, and modern versions of this design classic are still produced today. The sleek appearance, stackable shape, and modern composition of this dining chair insure it is very much part of the contemporary home.

These, and other such wonderfully designed pieces, along with the bold use of diverse materials, give the contemporary house the sense of style for which it is known.

The contemporary house knows no boundaries. Walls give way to open-plan design and the space created is used to its best advantage, providing a perfect showcase for a thoroughly modern interior.

SPACES

And the walls came tumbling down

The one word most often used to describe the contemporary house is spacious. Somehow these light, bright houses always seem to have an abundance of floor space. But take a tape measure to them, and you'll find this isn't always the case. Unless you own a house that has been designed and built to larger-than-average specifications, there's a strong possibility that your house is actually confined within the walls of what is either an old house, a converted building split into several apartments, or a modern block of apartments. All of these are places that put some form of constraint on the dimensions of the living space available.

The main reason why the contemporary house appears to be so spacious is that maximum use has been made of all the available living space. In fact, the most characteristic feature of the contemporary house is that it is actually devoid of many features, particularly those common in older properties, such as deep baseboards, cove molding, alcoves, and fireplaces. The stark use of space in the contemporary house, where all the boundaries have been pushed back, insures that every available inch of wall and floor area is made use of, and this results in a large, modern interior. Since baseboards and cove molding have often not been installed at all, or have been removed, the walls, ceiling, and floor may meet without any decorative feature to finish the join. Some contemporary homes are being built with these period features

below A terra-cotta urn, lit by a spotlight from above, makes an attractive display in this alcove.

right A distressed wooden dining table is very much at home here, the blue surface echoing the color of the kitchen cabinets. The upholstered dining chairs provide elegant shapes and comfort at the table.

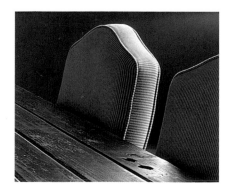

above *Perhaps the most captivating feature of this room is the curved yellow wall, with its two alcoves for display. However, the use of wood—both old, for the table, and new, for the floor—makes an interesting contrast.*

incorporated into the design, but they are the exception rather than the rule and the features tend to be less ornate than those found in period homes.

In many new contemporary developments, the fashion is for an open-plan interior, so dividing walls simply aren't put up in the first place. Similarly, old buildings not originally intended for habitation, such as factories, warehouses, and schools, are converted in a way that replicates New York loft-living styles— where one large open area is used for living and working, with perhaps just the bathroom, and maybe the bedrooms, separated off for privacy. In many traditional homes dividing walls are being taken down to open up the space, in particular in the living area. The most common practice is to remove the wall between the dining and living rooms, which results in a more spacious feel because the light from the windows at both ends of the house can pass through into the extended room. Other changes that can make quite a difference to the space are removing the wall that separates the entrance hall from one or two downstairs rooms, or opening up the kitchen into the dining area. Each of these modifications increases the amount of light that passes through an interior, which is one of the main ways of making it feel a lot more spacious. You'll notice too that in most contemporary homes windows are usually left bare to allow the maximum flow of light, as some blinds, shades, and curtains can restrict the amount of light entering the room. The absence of window treatments also helps create the streamlined interior design scheme for which the contemporary house is known.

The light fantastic

If you're daunted by the prospect of removing walls within the home, which can be costly, or in some cases is not a suitable option, there are other ways to maximize light and the feeling of space within a room. The cheapest and fastest method of creating a sense of increased space is to paint all your interior walls white. Immediately the room will look clean, bright, and

above *The utilitarian metal chairs around the dining table are matched by the kitchen stools.*

opposite *Glass, metal, and wood combine perfectly to create a stylish interior. The clever use of spotlights also creates an extremely eye-catching design.*

spacious, because the paler your walls, the more they will appear to "recede," whereas the darker they are, the more they will seem to close in. For the best results go for white walls, and a white ceiling. Use a latex velvet rather than flat latex paint because latex velvet has a slightly reflective sheen when it dries, unlike flat latex, which is matte. This brings us on to the other reason why a room painted white seems spacious, and that is because white reflects light. Any reflection of light within a room will give the interior a more spacious feel.

Mirrors are an excellent way to increase the amount of light within a room. Ideally they should be positioned to catch the light as it falls through the window and to reflect it around the room. There are many tricks you can perform with mirrors, from simply placing a mirror on the wall in the traditional way to covering one whole wall with sheet mirror, which will visually double the size of the room. This is why mirrored closet doors along the length of one wall in the bedroom of small modern homes are so popular. Until recently this idea was seen as a little *passé*, but now the full-wall mirror is enjoying a revival in contemporary interiors. In the bathroom or the powder room, a full-wall mirror will double the apparent size of what is often quite a small room, and the results are easier to live with in a room that you're not using all the time. As an alternative, one mirrored wall along a hallway can help to reflect light in what can often be a dark area. It will also increase its size visually.

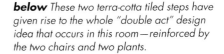

below *These two terra-cotta tiled steps have given rise to the whole "double act" design idea that occurs in this room—reinforced by the two chairs and two plants.*

right *These plain cotton slipcovers used over the directors' chairs are very simple but stylish.*

below *Despite being based on a white and terra-cotta color scheme, this spacious room is far from boring thanks to the use of plants, flowers, and the clever "double act" design idea.*

above *This striking black and white room is prevented from being too austere by the use of wood. Flashes of gold which reflect the wood can be seen throughout the room in the pillows, rug, and choice of flowers.*

Glass is, therefore, frequently the material of choice in the contemporary home. Large plate-glass windows are an obvious choice, and if it is possible to incorporate them into your home, then do so— they will maximize the amount of light available. Rebuilding a wall from floor to ceiling with a picture window can look fantastic, providing privacy isn't an issue. However, altering the size of your windows isn't a simple task, so changes to the interior using glass are usually an easier option. A window wall allows two areas to remain divided but still lets light pass through. Used between the entrance hall and living area, or to divide the kitchen and dining spaces, especially if removal of a whole wall isn't possible, a window wall can be a very effective option. Of course, there are always safety concerns with glass, particularly when children are around. Use toughened or preferably laminated glass.

Glass bricks have come into their own in recent years. Once the preserve of public buildings, these building blocks are increasingly finding their way into contemporary interiors. A wall, be it interior or exterior, made from these blocks gives a building an exciting edge, not only helping to increase the sense of light, but also adding interest as a design feature. Glass bricks can be used very successfully in fairly small quantities to build a simple structure such as a shower enclosure, a small wall to separate a utility area from the main kitchen/dining area, or a bathroom within a bedroom.

below *This white uplight placed between the two windows is unobtrusive thanks to its shape and color which allow it to blend in seamlessly.*

right *An overpacked bookcase can look messy, but by selecting books with predominantly white spines, and displaying them in both vertical and horizontal piles, this is avoided.*

Room for movement and improvement

Despite the modern, strong graphic designs and features in the contemporary house, there is also a certain fluidity to be found. This fluidity comes primarily from the way in which space is divided up in the modern interior. Living areas, or indeed any area that relies on furniture rather than structural features to denote its use, need never be static. It is this capacity for change that makes contemporary homes so attractive. You know what each space is used for by the furniture that appears within it, but this needn't be a permanent arrangement. A dining area can be created by placing the dining table close to the windows during the summer, or can be moved to a cozy corner in the winter. In this way you can enjoy the different living possibilities offered by one room, according to the dictates of the season. Similarly, a relaxation area is simply created in the main living space by arranging a comfortable sofa or armchairs around a rug. Lamps or other low-level lighting help contribute to the mood.

Notice too that in most contemporary-style homes the furniture isn't pushed back against the wall, but more often is grouped in the center of the room—a direct contrast to traditional furniture arrangements and one that results in a much more modern look.

opposite This room looks light and spacious thanks to the unbroken expanse of wooden floor and the large, plain plate-glass windows.

above *Rays of sunlight streaming through the Venetian blinds make a wonderfully graphic striped pattern on the wall, enhancing this split-level room.*

In the contemporary house there is usually no permanent method of separating the living and dining areas. Subtle approaches such as the use of lighting, choice of flooring, or arrangement of pieces of furniture will indicate the change of use of an area within a room. Semi-permanent divisions can include screens, panels, or sliding doors. More permanent divisions can include walls—but not necessarily in the traditional sense, as half-height walls are a popular way of creating a division that still allows light to travel across an area. This gives the best of both worlds. Another permanent division is through the use of railings. Railings allow light to travel through the space and allow all areas of the home to be seen, while still creating a boundary.

Split-level living is one of the defining features of the contemporary house. In its simplest form this can mean just a couple of steps separating two different areas, while visually the space remains a whole. Creating a false floor is not particularly difficult structurally, so steps can be quite easily incorporated into the interior design scheme. Raising one particular area can make a huge impact, thrusting an otherwise unremarkable space into

below *The many warm and varied tones of this wood floor are visually interesting. The idea of stripes is reflected throughout the room in the lines of the steps and the blinds.*

right *Wooden Venetian blinds are an excellent choice as you can carefully control the amount of light and privacy they provide.*

the forefront of the design. If your property is split-level, it is important that you make the most of it. Hiding, shielding, or disguising areas that may be exposed via the steps is such a waste—you need to be able to see into the next living space and to appreciate what it has to offer. In more traditional homes you can help create a split-level feel by opening up staircases and using railings, glass walling, or other transparent or semi-opaque materials. On the upper levels of the house, removing part of a paneled staircase can result in a gallery-like effect, which allows you to see down to the floor below. If your home features particularly high ceilings, then it may be possible to create a mezzanine level between floors. This new gallery space can be put to many uses. It's ideal for a home office, a dining space, or perhaps a relaxation area where a TV, music system, and soft low-level seating or floor pillows are all that's required.

Clean living

Contemporary homes are informal, but never sloppy or untidy. There's certainly no place for clutter, because each item of furniture needs to stand out and be admired in its own right. The absence of clutter is one of the main reasons the contemporary home always looks so spacious. All the decorating tricks or clever approaches to layout and lighting won't mean a thing if the end result is obscured by lots of furniture and enough clutter to rival a garage sale. Homes need furniture, but they only really need

opposite This modern apartment boasts a mezzanine level and includes some radical design ideas such as lively geometric wallpaper chosen to echo the design of the kitchen flooring.

below The wooden stairs have a white painted border making the staircase appear narrower than it really is. Although not very practical in this position, the gerberas make an effective design statement.

right This dramatic black and white floor marks out the kitchen area, and was also the inspiration behind the choice of wall covering in this modern apartment.

above This room has been designed so that the outdoors and indoors appear to merge. The wooden floor is echoed by the deck outside, and the trees are reflected in the choice of wicker, rattan, and wooden furniture throughout the room.

certain pieces. A judicious approach is what's required. It's important that you think hard about what you actually *need*, rather than go for everything that you *want*. Otherwise, you could end up with a busy interior that destroys the feeling of light and space you have so carefully created by opening up the home and using reflective materials and colors. The same measured approach should be taken when choosing accessories—one or two pictures on the wall are fine, but any more and you're at risk of becoming cluttered. Likewise, you must be very selective when choosing collectibles—try to avoid buying too many "dust collectors." It is far better to have one exquisite piece that's a real talking point than half a dozen run-of-the-mill items. Many contemporary furniture pieces and accessories can actually be quite expensive. Given that less is more, you can justify these costs quite easily!

Family homes in particular need storage facilities, but in the contemporary home you should try to keep items behind closed doors. A couple of closets in the entrance hall, a small spare room, or a large attic can be used to keep essentials. A modern interior demands a puritanical approach to possessions, and only those items that you put to regular use should be rewarded with closet or shelf space of their own. Shelves may feature in the living room, but on the whole they are intended for display purposes only—a vase here, a stack of books there. If you really must have more than this, it is imperative that you set out the items in the most efficient way possible. Tidily arrange a row of CDs or matching photo albums, or use smaller decorative storage boxes to group items together—but avoid a higgledy-piggledy pile of odds and ends on the shelves.

below *A plant displayed in a large wicker basket brings elements of the outdoors into this contemporary home.*

above *The pillows and sofa are covered in an attractive heavy-weave fabric that adds an organic quality to the room.*

All manner of materials have a place in the contemporary house. Whether used in the traditional or a more inspired modern way, the variety of textures and finishes insures that every functional item acquires a unique form.

MATERIALS

The diversity of materials used in the contemporary house is one of the things that make these homes so interesting and visually appealing. Take a look around a typical contemporary interior and in just one area you will find up to half a dozen building materials incorporated into the design. The materials may range from the more traditional types that have stood the test of time, such as wood, glass, or terra-cotta, to modern contenders such as metal, rubber, or plastic. One of the reasons these materials strike such a strong note is that the places where you will find them are not always where you'd expect. Brick walls in the living room or metal surfaces in the kitchen, for example, are becoming commonplace. Rubber, leather, or metal flooring is also increasingly finding its niche.

Building blocks

Look around any modern city and you will see many offices, shops, and even some homes built from materials other than traditional wood, brick, or stone. Step inside these buildings and you'll find the most splendid interiors—from the intensely urban, where metal is used for staircases, floors, or even walls, to light and spacious buildings where glass is the material of choice for walls, stairs, and even elevators. Much of the inspiration for the contemporary house has it roots in industry and the utilitarian

opposite This contemporary kitchen is made up of a variety of interesting materials including wood, metal, ceramic tile, plastic, glass, and even wicker.

below An organic granite countertop and translucent plastic storage jars can be successfully combined.

right The textured glass in the doors of these kitchen cabinets is visually appealing, and it's also practical since it allows the cabinets' contents to be partially seen.

below *The warm tones of wood and brick contrast well with the modern metallic Venetian blind and the plain cream canvas upholstery. The bright modern art on the walls adds a lively burst of color that really enhances the room.*

right *Plain brick walls, with their variations in color and texture, are very much in vogue in the contemporary interior.*

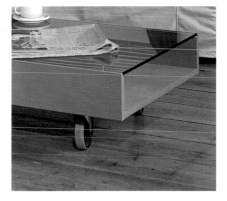

above *Reclaimed wood, wood veneer, and glass are all part of the contemporary home—as is furniture that can be rolled around to different positions.*

materials of offices and factories. Materials closely associated with industry have been admired and selected for use in the domestic interior not only because of the strong visual statement they make, but also for their practical, durable properties. After all, if they are used in public buildings these materials must surely be able to withstand the rigors of your home life. Similarly, given that so many contemporary interiors are used as home offices as well as living spaces, the industrial materials are particularly appropriate, mirroring developments in our approach to living and working.

Modern architects, such as Mies van der Rohe and Le Corbusier, loved using glass and steel for their buildings. Exposing the interior structure, which was a trademark of the Bauhaus school (see page 11), is an idea that has been embraced by the designers of contemporary houses, whose interiors display beams or metal joists and brickwork with pride. Likewise, Norman Foster is known as a hi-tech architect who is at home with these most contemporary of materials, as shown in some of his best-known buildings, such as the steel frame and glass Hong Kong and Shanghai Bank in Hong Kong and his glass additions to the new Reichstag building in Berlin.

Material gain

The key to combining successfully so many materials in the home is to select each one for the beauty of its own particular characteristics, and not to make any attempt to disguise the

opposite *The addition of a brick alcove makes all the difference to this serene cream living room. Canvas shades filter the light, creating interesting shadows on the adjacent wall.*

material with paint, fabric, or accessories. Leave bricks bare—their rough textures and range of hues are there to be appreciated and will make a strong contribution to the overall design scheme.

Wood is a popular choice throughout the contemporary home—its use as a building material and for flooring and furniture is a testament to its versatility. Increasingly it's not only the best-quality hardwoods that are preferred; cheaper pine is very popular, as are wood-based options such as plywood, laminates, and even medium-density fiberboard. The beauty of the grain and color of wood means that it is invariably at its best in its natural state, without being painted over, although applying a coat of varnish or wax to increase its durability is a good idea. Pale woods such as pine, beech, maple, and ash are particularly good for contemporary floors—the paler the surface, the larger the area covered appears to the eye, and the more light is reflected. Avoid dark woods such as oak, walnut, and mahogany, as their dense, heavy appearance doesn't sit well in modern surroundings.

Many of the most popular contemporary materials have been around for years and their use in the home is hardly new. What is new and original is the way in which these materials are now being used. Glass was long confined to windows, but in the 20th century began to be used for furniture, particularly tabletops and shelves. More recently glass has become a fairly common building material, with sheet glass and glass blocks being popular design features of contemporary homes. The smooth, easy-to-clean surface of glass makes it a perfect choice for a streamlined design, and its transparent quality means it helps increase the feeling of light and space, which is so paramount in the design of modern interiors. Its use on stairways is beginning to be seen too, even though the cost of building a glass staircase can be high, as a result of the technical planning and construction work involved.

below *Many modern materials can be found in this kitchen including stainless steel, tubular steel, hammered metal on some of the drawer fronts, and wrought iron for a door handle. The gray and blue color scheme enhances the gray metal tones.*

left *These metal bar stools with their black leather seats are the perfect complement to the dark tones of the granite breakfast bar, supported by two tubular steel legs.*

Metals

Metal has stamped its personality firmly on the contemporary house—in kitchen cabinets, staircases, furniture, even flooring. It is a perfect example of how a material with its roots in an industrial environment has been adopted for use in the modern home. Metal furniture first started appearing in homes in the 1930s. Today metal is seen in other parts of the home too. Treadplate flooring can be found in factories all over the country and its popularity is steadily growing within the domestic environment. Treadplate metal floor tiles are readily available, which makes the laying of this product easier. It is most effective in the kitchen, but if you want something really cutting edge then use it throughout areas of high wear.

Stainless-steel kitchen cabinets, once the preserve of catering establishments, are now another kitchen mainstay. Their strong, practical, easy-to-clean, and stain-resistant surface makes them an ideal choice for a utilitarian kitchen. If you find the hard lines of stainless steel too harsh then why not use matte brushed steel as an alternative (see page 58, where it is used as a very striking modern frame for a mirror). Aluminum is another metal popular in the contemporary house. Used more for furniture and accessories than for floors or kitchen surfaces, this metal is very much at home in modern surroundings, and its silvery white

below *Modern in both material and shape, a triangular cooktop hood makes a stylish statement in this contemporary kitchen.*

below *Old and new are successfully combined here — the fireplace harks back to a more traditional style of home but is brought right up to date with the use of concrete and the part-concrete flooring. This is a great example of how the modern and the organic can be used together, and the plain cream walls insure that all the materials are seen to their best advantage.*

right This metal mesh covering is a striking design feature and shows how a quite radical addition can look perfectly at home in a neutral setting.

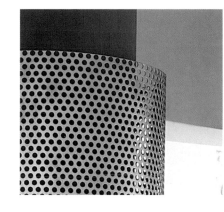

above A rattan basket works well with the other natural and textural materials in the room and provides the ideal receptacle for magazines and papers that could otherwise clutter the space.

metallic surface is reflective and practical. Look out for aluminum trash cans, dish racks, and shelving systems in utilitarian designs that can transform the feel of your kitchen.

Concrete

Ever since Frank Lloyd Wright designed New York's exciting Solomon R. Guggenheim museum in concrete, this material has been associated with both the exterior and the interior of the contemporary house.

Concrete floors have become very fashionable. A plain one can look striking, or it can be painted, stained, or even sandblasted to create pattern. If you are having a concrete floor laid, you could make it look more interesting by adding color to the concrete mix, or by insetting ceramic tiles. As an alternative to poured concrete—or to use along with it—consider concrete paving slabs, which are available in a variety of sizes, shapes, textures, and colors. To prevent the floor from staining or producing dust, applying a few coats of sealant is advisable; this will create an attractive, slightly polished appearance. Concrete has been given a new lease on life not only as a practical flooring material but also as a material from which home furnishings are cast. It is now possible to find items of furniture such as seats and tables made from concrete, as well as accessories such as vases, dishes, and wine racks.

Natural winners

"Organic" is an important concept in contemporary styling, and the organic materials so popular in today's domestic setting reflect our general enthusiasm for all things natural. Although the contents of the homes featured in this book may be highly stylized and up-to-the-minute in appearance, the majority of materials used in them, whether for flooring, furniture, upholstery, or window treatments, are organic in nature rather than being purely man-made. This is why leather, suede, hide, rubber, and rattan, along with fabrics such as muslin, cotton, linen, burlap, silk, and wool all have a place. They are materials with a long history that, in the contemporary home, have been given a new lease on life through innovative design and an imaginative approach.

Leather was once used only for upholstery. In recent years, however, it has made its mark as a floor and wall covering, albeit an expensive choice. Not only does it feel soft and luxurious, but it is very good at deadening sound. Interestingly, leather has shaken off the slightly tacky image it had in the 1980s and has become a highly fashionable interior fabric, as shown by the imposing leather daybed opposite.

Rubber is also becoming increasingly popular as a highly durable floor covering—its practical nature has long been appreciated on the floors of industrial buildings. Rubber can be given a very modern finish, as it can be successfully dyed in a wide range of colors, including strong primary shades. It is available in various textures, particularly ribs and studs.

If a leather or rubber floor seems just a bit too radical, why not choose one of the beautiful natural materials such as seagrass, coir, or jute that have become so popular for the floor. The wonderful tactile quality of these materials is at the heart of their appeal. They look particularly good when teamed with brick or rough textures. Or use a heavily textured rug to contrast with a smooth, pale wood floor. Rattan, wicker, cane, and bamboo have a similar tactile organic appeal. They are either woven into

below *Leather has shaken off its slightly dreary image and is now a serious contender in the contemporary house. Hard-wearing, smooth, and sensuous, leather has an allure that is hard to beat.*

above *The open weave of this mesh metal chair provides a refreshing contrast to the dense, dark appeal of leather.*

below *Pale wood predominates in this clean, fresh interior. Not only does it contrast well with the beams in the ceiling, but it is also the perfect backdrop for the visual impact of the leather daybed.*

fascinating shapes for furniture, or used to make lightweight blinds and screens that let light filter through. Bamboo also makes a very attractive, durable flooring.

Skin deep

While leather and to a certain extent suede have been popular for a number of decades as furnishing fabrics, gracing sofas and chairs in particular, the appearance of hide is one of the most striking recent developments in contemporary fabrics. What is remarkable about this is that animal hide is just about as basic and as primitive a material as you can get, yet it is being used in the most modern, hi-tech homes. It is precisely this type of contrast that makes the contemporary house so exciting. It moves with the times, and its own rules of interior design evolve to take on new developments or to embrace materials that become available to the designer. Animal hides, such as goatskin and cowhide, are stunning for rugs, chair coverings (see the recliner on page 49), or large floor pillows.

Old dogs and new tricks

The juxtaposition of old and new is one of the keys to creating a thoroughly contemporary interior. A kitchen boasting old wooden beams is perfect when teamed with very modern stainless-steel units and halogen lighting (see page 31). Brick walls are often the originals, sandblasted when the property was remodeled or redesigned, and left unplastered.

There is a new approach to tiling too. Traditional designs have been replaced by the mix-and-match method of randomly tiling a surface with a range of solid-colored tiles in about half a dozen complementary colors. The inspiration for this new design idea, as seen on page 32, goes back thousands of years to the art of mosaic—another example of a traditional craft finding a happy niche in the contemporary interior. The idea of pattern in tiling has virtually been dispensed with—this new tiling technique offers an abstract form of pattern based more on color

opposite This wooden kitchen is given a contemporary feel by the addition of black appliances, tiles, and detailing such as the trim on the countertop and the tramline design on the floor.

left *Natural floor coverings such as sisal, jute, coir, and seagrass, despite being organic in origin, all have a place in the contemporary house.*

combinations than on intricate design. As such it ties in with the large, plain expanses that characterize the contemporary house. In many cases ceramic tiling has been replaced altogether by a more contemporary, industrial material, and it's quite common to find kitchen backsplashes, for example, made from a sheet of laminate, Plexiglas, or metal.

Keep an open mind as to how and where different materials can be used in the home. Pay homage to the past but keep one eye firmly on innovative design developments. Mix organic with industrial and you'll be well on the way to achieving an exciting contemporary home.

opposite *Metal and glass are the main contributors to this modern interior. The abstract light fixture provides a wonderful contrast to the straight lines of the mirror and chair frames.*

Nowhere else will you see such avant-garde, modern, or graphic shapes combined so successfully. Their bold combinations give rise to the stylish designs for which the contemporary house is known.

SHAPES

The focus on shapes is an important characteristic of the contemporary home. Although the majority of designs you will find incorporated in these interiors are very graphic, with straight edges and hard angles, there is almost without fail a softer, curved element included in the design of each room. It's this soft angle that catches the eye and gives a more human element to the whole scheme.

Shapes work a lot harder in a modern, open-plan setting, because there is so much less in the space to distract the eye. Because we are more aware of them, it is important that the shapes we choose and the way in which we use them are planned to perfection. Without the curving element provided by interesting and unusual shapes, the contemporary interior can run the risk of appearing somewhat harsh and stark.

In all the rooms shown here, close attention has been paid to the method by which shapes are introduced into the overall design scheme. The easiest way to include a shape is by adding it via furniture and accessories. However, if you can be involved in the grassroots stages of the design of your home, then why not think "shapes" in your approach to flooring, tiling, or work surfaces? Think about the exterior too. You could take your inspiration from the shape and form of the exterior, and carry this theme into the interior through the arrangement of furniture and the shapes of individual objects. Think about the wonderful spiral art space in the Solomon R. Guggenheim museum in New York, designed by Frank Lloyd Wright. It is the perfect casing for the modern art that it houses.

The learning curve

Contemporary houses are known for their audacious designs based on strong graphic shapes. These neat lines create order and discipline in the room, which is essential because the notion of neatness is important right through from the architectural planning stage to the care of personal possessions. You should avoid mess, clutter, and confusion on any level as this detracts from

right What is actually quite an ordinary kitchen is enhanced by an imposing semicircular table with a triangular base.

the principles of open-plan living and destroys the unique character of the contemporary home.

All the rooms in this chapter feature at least one curved item quite prominently, which contrasts with and complements the straight, graphic lines of the main design scheme. The recliner on page 49 is one such item. With its curved chrome frame it makes a huge impact in an ordered, uncluttered room. Clean, straight lines are found in the horizontals of the slats in the Venetian blinds and in the stripes in the rug on the floor. Even the brick wall adds to the graphic element because the rows of bricks also form lines. But the choice of the recliner and the jaunty angle at which it is positioned create a huge amount of interest and diversity within the room.

The curves you choose to include in your contemporary house can come from a variety of sources, be it the curve of the arm or seat of a chair or sofa, the round seat of a bar stool or tabletop, the gentle arc of a cooktop hood or rounded edge of a fridge door. The presence of at least some curved element is absolutely essential to give the contemporary home a degree of visual comfort, and it's not at all difficult to introduce this via your choice of furniture or furnishings. A home built on harsh, straight edges and angles alone can appear cold and unwelcoming. One well-chosen curving item is all it takes to balance the scheme.

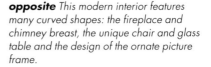

opposite *This modern interior features many curved shapes: the fireplace and chimney breast, the unique chair and glass table and the design of the ornate picture frame.*

right *The smooth pebbles in the fireplace with their rounded shape cleverly echo some of the curved design details within the room.*

Balancing act

To make a contemporary house symmetrical is perhaps taking modern ideas too far, but you do need to adopt a balanced approach to decorating. This can be achieved through the layout of the room and the positioning of furniture, right down to how shelves are filled and the placing of accessories around the room. The accessories may be minimal but the few items on show have to be carefully positioned so they can be seen to their best advantage, as well as to make the greatest impact. Notice how in the kitchen on page 62 a row of water bottles and glasses is used to fill a shelf. This display works because it is well balanced, and an attractive feature is made out of just four bottles and four glasses. More of one and less of another and the humor and effect of this arrangement would be lost. Likewise, on page 61 the shelves with their slanting uprights display a few items in an arrangement that is in perfect balance. Elsewhere in this book you can see other good examples of the balanced approach to contemporary interior design, such as in the three identical halogen lights that hang over the work surface in the kitchen on page 31. The success of these arrangements is in getting the balance right.

Once you have established which shapes will add interest to your room it is important that you don't get carried away

below *This plastic chair with its curved back and quite pointy arms offers a modern take on a traditional chair shape.*

below *This stunning, shapely sofa makes a superb contrast against the grid design of the window. The coffee table, with its curving, triangular-shaped legs and glass top, also adds interest to this interior.*

and create overkill. One shapely chair looks great, two may complement each other, but three or more in different designs will ruin the whole effect as each vies for attention. You should bear this in mind when considering any item that you may require more than one of—dining chairs, for example. If you're dealing in multiples then stick to the same design for the sake of unity, otherwise the end result will look messy and conflicting. Notice how two similar urns are used for display in the alcoves of the curved wall on page 15. No more than two of these items are needed for the balance you are trying to achieve.

The living area on page 19 is particularly noteworthy—the fabric-covered chairs and two miniature trees have all been carefully chosen to balance with the two steps in the room. Together these items make a clever visual reference to each other, the angles of the chairs set against the curve of the steps and the roundness of the plants demonstrating how diverse shapes can work together in harmony.

The shape of things to come

Shapes that mimic other shapes within the room are very much in evidence in the contemporary house. It's this type of visual fun that helps make the interiors so appealing. Straight lines and hard angles are everywhere, from the shape of the room and windows to the kitchen cabinets and the arrangement of pictures on the wall. This repetition enforces the modern approach to interior design, while at the same time alluding to other, similar designs within the room. Notice how on page 51 a circular fruit bowl is placed on top of a semicircular table, and on page 49 how the stripes in the rug echo those of the Venetian blinds at the windows, while on page 59 the glass sink's rounded shape is reflected by the shape of the mirror on the wall. A really fantastic play on shapes can be seen in the room on page 52, where a fireplace has been set in the corner of the room. The chimney breast itself is curved, and placed nearby is a mesh metal chair which, with its stylish seat/leg form, cleverly echoes the shapes of

opposite *A custom-made curved cabinet houses the fridge-freezer. The use of curved shapes is continued through the choice of bar stools and fruit bowl.*

the fireplace and chimney breast, resulting in an impressive visual harmony. Likewise, the nine small pictures hung on the wall on page 74 contrast nicely, and somewhat humorously, with the one large canvas that leans against the wall.

Generally speaking, in the contemporary interior man-made materials are used for the harder, more angular shapes within the rooms and natural fabrics for the softer shapes and curves. But there are some fantastic examples that contradict this rule, such as coiled tubular radiators; with their spring-like appearance, they combine the hardness of metal with a succession of attractive curves. These radiators are great fun, and their popularity means they are available from furniture stores and bathroom retailers at reasonable prices. Similarly, metal surfaces in the kitchen can be cut to a curved shape. This looks very appealing and the gentle design encourages movement and flow within the kitchen area, balancing the design and making the space feel more homey and relaxed.

The floor too has become a good place to try out an innovative approach to shape and design. Vinyl, linoleum, and carpet tiles are now available in all sorts of wonderful shapes, and many designs can be inlaid in the floor by the clever use of these materials. In this way curves can be incorporated into the very fabric of your home, not just added via furniture and furnishings.

Don't be nervous about going against the grain. As well as experimenting with curves in metals, for example, think about trying "soft" furnishings in hard fabrics. How about a cube stool

in metal or glass rather than suede or fake fur? After all, you're the only one making the decisions.

Fantastic furniture

Unusually shaped furniture is a mainstay of the contemporary house. Since there are often only a few items on show it is important that what items there are provide drama and interest. What you won't find are any details that break up the clean design lines of these pieces, so ruffles, pleats, or any other "decorative flourishes" are out. Take a look around and what you will see is furniture perhaps with unusual legs, an asymmetrical design, an interesting curve, or another design deviation from the norm. It is these alternative aspects of design that give character to the furniture found in the contemporary house. One of the great things about contemporary shapes is that you are limited only by your own imagination. Take it as far as you want to, and have some fun.

Humour was certainly on the agenda when one of the most striking pieces of furniture of recent years, the Mae West Hot Lips sofa based on a painting by Dalí, was designed. Put a piece of furniture like this in a room and its shape and color speak volumes. Similarly, the "Boxing Glove" chaise longue designed by the ground-breaking Swiss De Sede company really packs a punch. How about looking beyond the straight vs. curve dynamic and using fantastically shaped accessories, such as a spiky foam cube, a zigzag metallic CD rack, or a concrete ball?

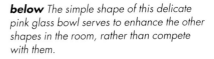

below *The simple shape of this delicate pink glass bowl serves to enhance the other shapes in the room, rather than compete with them.*

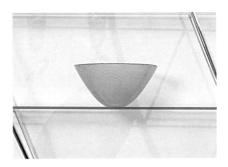

right *Even this vase has an interesting shape—its triangular appearance can be seen from both the top and the sides.*

above *Positioned so that the uprights are at a slant rather than exactly vertical, this set of shelves takes on a whole new dimension which very much adds to the overall appeal of the room.*

If you don't feel at home with such radical designs (and don't forget, you may later), a simple curve along the back of a sofa, the rounded shape of a tube chair, or an easel-shaped table can provide a good deal of interest and will certainly give a modern twist to your home, without grabbing the attention as forcefully as some of the more fantastic pieces.

The comfort zone

Ergonomics is a word that is heard a great deal in connection with all types of furniture, from office essentials such as computer tables, keyboards, and chairs (which, of course, may well feature in your home, as living/working areas are becoming so common) to domestic items, particularly chairs. Ergonomically designed furniture results in stylishly shaped pieces the purpose of which is to provide support and comfort for the user. As such they are perfect for the contemporary home. A wooden or plastic dining chair with a slightly molded seat is so much more comfortable to sit on for long periods than one that has a completely flat surface. Chairs that are curved in the spine area are aesthetically pleasing as well as comfortable. Even a simple ergonomic design like the curve of a handle on a cabinet door can make all the difference, as it's these subtle approaches to design that grab our attention in an uncluttered space.

Remember, when thinking about shapes don't put aesthetics above comfort, unless you are choosing an object purely for its decorative appeal and do not require it to have any practical function whatsoever. This is particularly important for sofas and chairs. Try them out for comfort. At the end of the day, however important design is in the contemporary house, you'll always have made a bad investment if you purchase something you don't actually enjoy using, no matter how great it looks.

above *You couldn't get much simpler than this: a lineup of bottles and glasses purely for decorative effect. The result, however, is very striking.*

above *A row of modern storage jars reinforces the curved theme in this kitchen.*

opposite *A few well-chosen curves—found in the fridge, oven, and cooktop hood—are just enough to give this kitchen contemporary appeal.*

Color is used to great effect in the contemporary house. Often subtle, sometimes bold and bright, color adds a twist to an interior while enhancing the beautiful plain expanses of these truly modern homes.

COLOR SCHEMES

Dream color schemes

A contemporary house shows off its best features with a fairly simple color scheme. Again, we are back to space and light—a riot of colors will destroy the feel you are trying to achieve. When you first step into a contemporary home, it is easy to think that the space is plain and devoid of color. In fact, there is more to a contemporary color scheme than meets the eye. As you can see from the beautiful rooms featured in this chapter, color is not absent, it is simply used in a more subtle way than in many period homes. The contemporary house has evolved from the Modernist ideal, and although the majority of these interiors may be restrained in their approach to decoration, there is usually a big splash of color in some form that jazzes up the room, creating a focal point and adding interest. There are two main color schemes generally associated with the contemporary house. One is a scheme based on neutrals, while the other is one made up of bright colors. However, when you take a look at the rooms shown here you'll find that many of the houses boast color schemes that are actually a mix of both.

Given the minimalist appearance of most contemporary houses, you could be forgiven for thinking that little effort has gone into the design of the color scheme. After all, what can be so difficult about painting a room white and placing a red sofa in it? In reality, however, it can be more difficult to make a plain and

opposite *This is a fairly subtle combination of blues, greens, yellows, and neutrals. The light shade of blue used for the walls helps maximize the feeling of light and the room is given individuality by the modern painting and the punchy tartan sofa.*

below *Curved metal legs give an elegant shape to these contemporary chairs.*

right *Furniture on casters is a must for an open-plan living area. The easily moveable furniture allows you to give a different feel to specific areas of the space.*

above This plain white color scheme is enhanced by judicious splashes of color: the turquoise chairs are teamed against a royal blue wall and the black sofa is livened up by the addition of bright pink pillows.

simple color scheme interesting, because we worry that it could fall into the category of being "dull." In fact, the secret is to exercise restraint and understand that a scheme which in a period house could well be considered uninteresting, in a contemporary house will actually add to the overall effect by bringing out the beauty of the strong materials and light-filled spaces.

When planning a color scheme for a contemporary house you need to look at all the elements in the room together. Don't make the mistake of isolating painting and decorating as a task to be carried out without reference to what is happening in the rest of the room. Look to the natural materials and take your inspiration from them. For example, wooden floors are very popular and can give rise to a color scheme based on the hues found within the wood. These may vary from pale blond colors to richer browns and beiges. Then look at the shades of brick. Brick offers the opportunity to develop a cream, terra-cotta, or even a golden-brown or fiery-orange scheme, while glass can take you in the direction of a gray, blue, or green design scheme. Identifying and developing schemes based on the materials found in the room takes some practice and imagination, but once you begin to feel at home with this approach you will be able to create some very inspiring and pleasing color schemes.

Basing a color scheme around your furniture or accessories is another option, and can be simpler because furnishings tend to be in more solid colors, so there is no confusion in identifying and picking out the correct shade in which to decorate. On page 78 a very modern and colorful ceiling light was all it took to inject some bright hues into an otherwise fairly plain room. The theme is continued in the upholstery of the six dining chairs, and with only a minimal addition of color the room is transformed from a plain white interior to one that appears quite rich and vibrant. The choice of a glass dining table is not accidental; it has been selected so as not to detract from this visual color play. The use of any other material for the table may well have competed for attention and prevented the chairs and light fixture from being the stars of the show.

below To distract attention from the windows, white curtains are used, because they blend in to the overall color scheme.

below *A neutral color scheme works well in a contemporary setting. Mixing several shades together adds interest, and an injection of bright colors can really pack a punch. This modern painting is all it takes to add an element of drama.*

Some contemporary homes actually boast quite adventurous color schemes. The difference is in the approach. Generally speaking, color schemes for the contemporary house are developed in a different way to those for more traditional homes. Often they are based on several shades of one color—an idea best illustrated by the blue kitchen on page 77, in which the turquoise cabinets are teamed with navy wall tiles and modern molded chairs to form a highly contrasting but very effective color scheme. A similar idea is shown on page 68, where the turquoise upholstered dining chairs are set against a distant wall painted royal blue.

below *Even the view over neutral-colored buildings, with no greenery to be seen, reinforces the plain color scheme.*

A whiter shade of pale

The simplest and still the most popular color for the contemporary home is white. A white room gives a clean, bright interior. As white reflects light so effectively, it helps a room appear at its largest, and looks modern, clinical, and functional. Any decorative features such as a cove or baseboards should be painted the same shade as the walls for continuity, and to make them as inconspicuous as possible. Highlighting and drawing attention to these architectural features isn't appropriate in the contemporary house.

Sometimes an all-white scheme may feel a little overpowering and on a practical level is not always easy to keep at its pristine

right *The warm honey tones of wood warm up a color scheme based on neutral shades.*

above Painting walls in different colors can look very appealing. Here the pastel shades of green and yellow complement each other perfectly, as do the differing wood tones.

best in a family home. Why not go for a neutral color scheme that takes its inspiration from the starkness of white, but adds a little warmth and variation? By modifying the shades of white throughout the room, introducing hues such as milk, cream, bone, and lace, you will create some interesting color schemes that complement the materials and furnishings found in the contemporary home. These schemes have become popular in recent years because they are light, reflective colors that help create the illusion of space by drawing back the walls and making rooms feel larger, and as such perform the same function as white. At the same time they give an extra dimension and interest to an interior that cannot always be achieved by white alone.

The popularity of neutral color schemes can be seen by looking at almost any paint chart, as there are easily half a dozen or more variations on white, each with a tiny hint of color, and plenty more in the beige and cream spectrum too. Many of these colors have names like Wheat, Barley, or Cane, which ties in with the use of organic materials in the contemporary home. These shades are developed to coordinate well with materials such as wood, rattan, linen, and stone. Clever use of neutrals allows you to vary the tone of a room enormously, while retaining a clean, spacious appearance. Think about what materials are in your home and choose your neutral shades accordingly. Grays work best to accentuate the feel and texture of concrete, metals, and stone, while creams or beiges can bring out the natural beauty of

below *All these surfaces work well next to each other. The wood partition with its rich cherry tones stands out against the more muted pastel shades.*

right *The tone of the pale maple table is just right against a pastel yellow wall.*

brick, wood, wicker, rattan, or terra-cotta. Why not take your organic or natural color scheme to its logical conclusion by using eco-friendly paints that are free of the chemicals and plastics that go into synthetic paints?

The color conundrum

The use of pastel colors is increasing throughout the contemporary house, but the modern pastel schemes are a far cry from the somewhat anemic color combinations of pink and gray or blue and yellow that were so popular in the 1980s. One reason pastel shades are in favor again is that some of the objects in these contemporary houses hark back to the design icons of the 1950s, particularly when it comes to kitchen appliances. The curved retro styling of fridges, countertops,

above *This simple plywood light shade with its square motif cleverly repeats the design idea created by the nine pictures on the wall.*

opposite *Designed around a pastel color scheme, this room looks clean, fresh, and modestly colorful. It is the perfect illustration of how pastels have an important place in the contemporary house.*

left *These pillows have been chosen to complement the pastel-colored panels leaning against the wall behind the chair, and the vivid purple lamp seen in the main picture.*

and kitchen stools is very popular in the contemporary kitchen. These pastel "ice cream" colors suit the mood conveyed by the '50s designs really well, and add a colorful twist to the contemporary scheme.

The trick when using color is to be imaginative, and be prepared to break the rules. Introduce a color on one wall only, rather than every wall. Colored wall panels are great because they allow you to add color to the room without letting it dominate. With panels a popular approach is to work to a neutral palette, and then pick out just one wall in a stronger tone of one of the neutral shades—perhaps a mocha as a strong contrast to a softer shade of beige, or an olive as a contrast to a pale eau de nil.

Some contemporary homes boast a much stronger burst of color in the form of acid brights or primary colors. These vivid shades work well, again in moderation, and look particularly dramatic when chosen for man-made materials such as metal or plastic. The general rule of thumb is that the stronger the color, the less of it is required to add impact. Although painting one wall in such an intense shade can work—a lively lime green makes a good background for mirrors and pictures with metal frames— their use is best restricted to furniture or accessories, so the color doesn't become too overpowering. Notice how in the rooms shown here often just a chair, a painting, or a pillow in one of these colors is all that is required. The impact is still strong.

Picture this—no patterns!

Take a look at almost any of the rooms featured here and you'll notice a distinct lack of pattern. Furniture and furnishings in the contemporary interior are plain, walls are devoid of wallpaper, and even the smallest accessories are chosen more for their color or shape than for their patterns or designs. You may find some pattern on a rug, a pillow, or a wall hanging, but its use is definitely restricted. Pattern is absent for the same reason as is a riot of color—it simply goes against the aesthetic of the contemporary home. If you are intent on using pattern, aim for

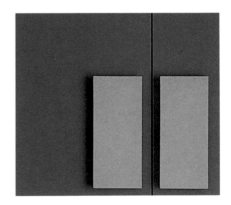

above *Large white laminate rectangles form the handles on the jade cabinets.*

below *It used to be said that blue and green should never be seen, but you have only to take a look at this kitchen to realize that turquoise and navy blue make an excellent combination.*

below *This light fixture really is the light fantastic, as it gives rise to the idea of upholstering the dining chairs in wonderful jewel-colored velvets and thereby creating a fabulous contemporary color scheme.*

right All the chairs in this room correspond to a color in the overhead light fixture, apart from the orange one, which is inspired by the uplight on the wall next to the shelves.

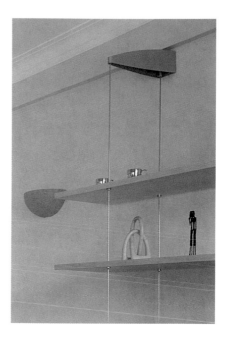

above The uprights for this modern shelving unit are formed from taut wire cables which pass through holes in the wooden shelves.

modern, graphic patterns—look to the work of 20th-century artists such as Kandinsky, Mondrian, Pollock, or Klee for your inspiration. Let the colorful abstract designs of Kandinsky, himself a lecturer at the Bauhaus school of design, or the rigorous abstract style of Mondrian, whose work is based on geometric shapes and primary colors, be your guide. Rugs, curtains, and upholstery fabrics that replicate some of the classic designs of these artists are becoming increasingly easy to find. Avoid fussy, detailed, or very ornate, old-fashioned patterns. These have no place in the contemporary house.

The art you choose for your walls is also very much a part of the overall design scheme in the contemporary house. The color content of your pictures should coordinate or very obviously contrast with your color scheme. It's best to choose from the modern art stable, as graphic images will compound the design ideas found within your home. Think twice before choosing a piece just because it is by your favorite artist—it may not be right for the feel of your home.

*Natural and man-made materials work together
in unique combinations enhancing the beautiful
furniture that they cover. Color and texture are
all-important, resulting in tactile pieces which
display great charm.*

FURNISHINGS AND FABRICS

right *Strange design details such as this stone water fountain can actually work well in the contemporary home.*

When it comes to furnishings and fabric, almost anything goes in the contemporary house and many different styles can find a happy home here. Fabrics fall into two camps: the very modern—plastic, nylon, and other synthetic materials—and the organic, such as animal hides, suede, leather, cotton, and linen. Never has such a diverse selection of fabrics been available for use. What you'll notice with these fabrics, with the exception of animal prints, is that pattern has no place among them. Nearly all the fabrics that feature in this book are plain. They rely on their shape, color, and texture to provide interest.

Take a seat

Contemporary furniture boasts svelte lines, interesting shapes, and great design. Here, "contemporary" is a relative term. Many of the pieces we consider to be the ultimate in cutting-edge design today in fact draw their inspiration from items designed over 70 years ago. The chair has always been one of the icons of modern design. Perhaps the best example is the "Wassily" chair, designed in 1925 by Marcel Breuer, another Bauhaus architect and designer. With its chromed tubular steel frame and taut leather straps that form the seat, back, and armrests, this chair displays many of the elements associated with contemporary style. Countless offices and homes possess at least one of these striking chairs.

Mies van der Rohe, also from the Bauhaus school, is another Modernist who has exerted a huge influence over contemporary

above *With its angular design this plain cream armchair contrasts well with the dramatic red sofa and leopard print chair. It's linked to the sofa by the red tasselled pillow.*

opposite *The decorative elements in this room—the trendy modern furniture, artwork, and lighting—are all enhanced by the white walls, wooden floor, and beamed ceiling.*

furniture design. He is most famous for his pieces designed from chromed tubular steel. You can see his influence in homes, offices, and stores, in the abundance of chrome tables, chairs, bed frames, and stools now available. Alvar Aalto, a Finnish architect and designer of huge influence, preferred furniture of a more organic origin. He designed many of his pieces for laminated bent plywood, which allows softer, more rounded shapes. The natural flexibility of the wood means that this furniture is self-sprung. Once again, his influence is all around us still. More recently, the French interior designer Philippe Starck has designed many items—from furniture to faucets— which have immediately become icons of the contemporary house. Likewise, the classic polypropylene chair of the 1960s is still widely available, several decades after it was originally designed.

Take a look at any current furniture catalogs and you'll see a whole host of pieces whose design has been influenced by these Modernist forebears. Don't think you need to go for the originals, which can be expensive, to achieve the look you are after. There are many mass-market options that adhere to the same design principles and use these iconic pieces as their inspiration but are far more affordable.

What makes these pieces from the past so in demand today is that their clean lines and well-designed shapes are almost impossible to improve upon. The contemporary house is based on slim, fine lines, and any bulky, busy, overdesigned items will ruin the gracious streamlined design that is essential to the character of the modern interior.

And so to bed...

Seating is just one example of where design is very important, but other major pieces need to be just as carefully considered if they are to work successfully in a modern setting. Beds are by their nature fairly large items, so attention to design is critical as they will inevitably be the focus of attention in the bedroom.

opposite *The hard surfaces of brick and wood are softened by the use of cream textiles such as the wool blanket, corduroy pillows, and cotton seat pad on the chair.*

above These dining chairs are based on Modernist design of the 1920s—their cantilevered form is inspired by the work of Mies van der Rohe, and the use of tubular steel comes from Le Corbusier.

This is not the place for bulky sprung bed frames; light-colored wood or modern metals such as brushed aluminum or tubular steel for frames are a far better choice. If you buy a bed that is slightly raised on legs to allow the floor to show underneath, this is ideal as it adds to the feeling of spaciousness within the bedroom. Whatever material you choose for your bed frame, its lines should be clean and simple and uncluttered by complicated designs. Bedlinen also works well in simple designs and neutral colors; bulky duvets or bedspreads can look clumsy in the contemporary interior. The bedrooms on pages 85 and 93 both look inviting yet neat, the white cotton sheets in the former softened by the addition of a Merino wool blanket. The simple pale wood bedsteads add understated interest to the rooms.

Storage pieces such as armoires also need to be simple in design. They will inevitably be large items, but any fussy design or heavy materials should be avoided. Again simple, unadorned, pale wood veneers are the best choices for door fronts, although glass (perhaps frosted so the contents are slightly obscured), metal mesh, or mirrors are other excellent choices that work well within the design brief. Door handles and knobs should be small and unobtrusive, and made from a material that is in keeping with the contemporary theme. Little leather tabs, small aluminum knobs,

below *This living/dining room may not look as starkly contemporary as some, but it boasts many modern design ideas and materials such as tubular steel, rattan, and animal hide, all within a less blatant setting.*

left This corner offers plenty of interest, from the zany chair to the busy display of art. The shelves, true to form in the contemporary house, are left uncluttered.

or just indentations within the door frames are all that are required. Attention to detail can make all the difference as to whether a piece works or not in the contemporary home.

And the living is easy

Your choice of occasional furniture can give an exciting new angle to a contemporary interior. Unlike beds, chairs, and tables, which may be subject to a great deal of use, smaller items such as shelves, coffee tables, bookcases, and footstools are used to a lesser degree. So although they must be robust enough to cope with the job for which they are designed, it is their form rather than their function that takes priority. Because these pieces cost less than a large item such as a bed, it's easier to acquire something with a great design that will make a dramatic statement in your home. Whether you go for a coffee table made from a single curved piece of plywood or from a concrete block, shelves from glass or from metal mesh, or a simple suede cube footstool, the important thing is to let the item bask in its own glory. Try not to hide it under books, newspapers, or accessories. It is the design and shape of these furnishings that help them pack a punch.

Casters are another popular feature. They not only raise the furniture and allow the space underneath to be seen, but their mobility offers the possibility of changing the feel of a space. In the contemporary home nothing should feel static, as the use of space can alter and change during the day, or at different times of the year. You need to have the means to implement change as the mood takes you, and roll-around furniture makes this easier.

Pure fabrication

To show the lines of contemporary furniture off to their best advantage you should opt for upholstery rather than covers. The look and feel of slipcovers, ruffles, pleats, or gathers clutters up the clean lines for which contemporary designs are known.

Upholstery fabrics include those that have stood the test of time, such as cotton, leather, or suede, as well as more modern

alternatives such as neoprene—a soft, spongy material that is more commonly used for making wetsuits—and tough polypropylene, the material used to make car seatbelts.

Animal-print furnishings have their roots way back. Popular in the 1930s and in Art Deco styling, they have cropped up throughout the decades in modern interiors, and have once again become fashionable in the contemporary home. The leopard-print chair on page 82 is teamed with a red sofa to make a stunning statement. These two items are all it takes to add real drama to the room. Recently, animal hides such as cow and pony skin have become popular for rugs or upholstery. The recliner chair on page 49 has been given a contemporary twist through the use of cowhide upholstery in the place of the original plain black leather.

There has been a noticeable improvement in the quality of fake furs over recent years, to the extent that it can be difficult to tell the fakes from the real thing. Throws and floor pillows made from these synthetic furs are popular. Using fake fur to upholster a chair is great fun and makes a soft, comfortable covering.

Many other fabrics with their roots in the past are also evident in the contemporary home—linen, hemp, cotton, and wool are all commonplace. Their organic qualities offer a natural element to a home that might otherwise be in danger of feeling too "synthetic." This is one of the main differences between today's contemporary look and the styles of the 1950s, '60s and '70s. The synthetic materials were the mainstay of modern interior design, whereas today the use of synthetics is restrained.

The juxtaposition of hard and soft is an element of design often repeated throughout the contemporary house. With the abundance of hard surfaces, balance is all important when planning your interior. Make sure hard surfaces are softened by the use of fabric—the hard lines of concrete furniture can be softened with a mohair throw, an expanse of wooden floor can be broken up with a rug, and the shiny leather surface of a sofa can benefit from the contrasting addition of one or two curly Mongolian sheepskin pillows.

opposite *Picking out just one wall and painting it a vibrant shade, then positioning a colorful, contrasting piece of modern furniture against it is all that's required to add pizzazz.*

The final curtain

Absence of clutter is what the contemporary interior is all about. Furnishings and fabrics that are not absolutely necessary are therefore often dispensed with. When it comes to window treatments, however, the line is slightly blurred. Bare windows are very much part of the overall look of the interior. Panes that are unhindered by curtains or shades allow the maximum amount of light into the room and may offer a view of a modern metropolis that reflects back the identity of the contemporary house. But there will always be times when you seek privacy, when the bright glare of the sun can be too much, or when insulation is needed, and this calls for some form of window treatment. The design should be as clean, as streamlined, and as unobtrusive as possible.

Blinds and shades are an obvious choice because they cover the window without adding bulk in the way traditional curtains can. Venetian blinds are popular in the contemporary house because they can be controlled to give as much light or as much privacy as you wish at different times during the day. The most modern versions come in metallic finishes—aluminum or metallic slats are ideal. Why not choose slats that are perforated with pinholes for added interest?

below *Voile curtains, crisp cotton sheets, and a modern take on the four-poster bed make for an elegant bedroom that looks cool, calm, and restful; it's based on an almost totally white color scheme.*

below *A rug used as a wall hanging positioned behind a black leather sofa provides the key design elements in this lounge. An emerald green carpet offers a colorful contrast. These deep colors are prevented from being overbearing because the large picture windows allow plenty of light to flood into the room.*

right *A state-of-the-art metal mesh table lamp makes an interesting addition to this room.*

above *An innovative table made from metal and glass and featuring a funnel-like fruit bowl at its center is perfect for the contemporary house in terms of both its material and its design.*

These blinds look particularly good in working areas such as kitchens, bathrooms, and home offices, because of the industrial origins of their materials. Wooden Venetian blinds work well too, though they are perhaps better suited to bedrooms and living rooms. They combine well with a wooden floor and come in a variety of wood finishes, so you can pick the shade that best suits the general color scheme of your home.

Roller shades are a versatile option. They give a lighter finish to the window, allowing you to expose the whole window easily. If privacy during the day isn't a major concern, roller shades may suit you. Choose them in the same color as your walls to provide continuity. Contemporary design details such as an aluminum bar, or a leather tab at the end of the shade, will keep it up-to-date and provide a link to the other materials featured in the room.

If you really cannot live without your curtains, at large sliding glass doors or on a window wall, for example, then make sure you keep them in as simple a style as possible. Avoid heavy fabrics, traditional pleated draperies, or details such as cornices. Opt instead for soft, lightweight fabrics such as organza, voile, or muslin. These delicate, floaty fabrics will hang in soft folds and diffuse the light, and their pure simplicity will complement the other materials and furnishings in the home.

PICTURE CREDITS

The author and publisher would like to thank Elizabeth Whiting Associates and the following photographers and organizations for their kind permission to reproduce photographs on the following pages: 2, 8, 10, 37, 68-9, 70-1, 74-5, 82-3, 88 Mark Luscombe-Whyte; 6, 40-1, 92-3 Tim Street-Porter; 9, 14-15, 18-19, 22, 28-9, 38-9, 47, 51, 65, 72-3, 90 Rodney Hyett; 13, 54-6, 86-7 Spike Powell; 16-17, 30-1, 34-5, 42-4, 48, 58-9, 85 Neil Davis; 20-1, 94-5 EWA; 24-5 Gerry Harpur; 26-7 Mark Nicholson; 32-3, 52, 76-7, 80 Tom Leighton; 46, 62-3 Di Lewis; 60-1 Nadia Mackenzie; 66-7 Nato Welson; 78-9 Tommy Candler.